Can You Eat Broccoli?

Seed
Learning

broccoli

spinach

lettuce

corn

carrots

onions

cucumbers

bell peppers

Can you eat broccoli?

Yes, I can eat broccoli.

Can you eat carrots?

Yes, I can eat carrots.

Can you eat corn?

Yes, I can eat corn.

Can you eat cucumbers?

Yes, I can eat cucumbers.

Can you eat lettuce?

Yes, I can eat lettuce.

Can you eat bell peppers?

Yes, I can eat bell peppers.

Let's learn more about Singapore.

Sambal stingray